I0479350

Happy Easter!

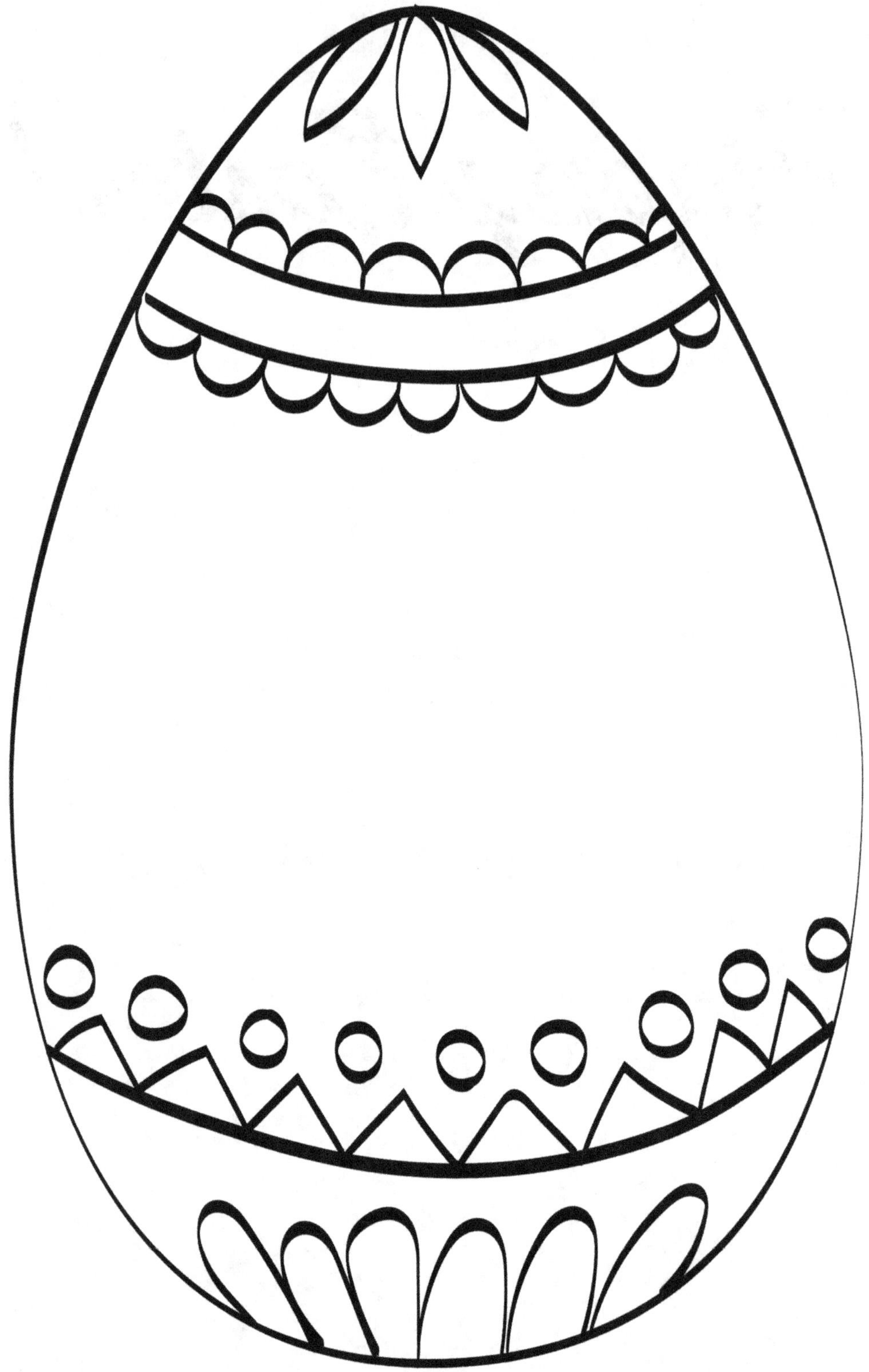

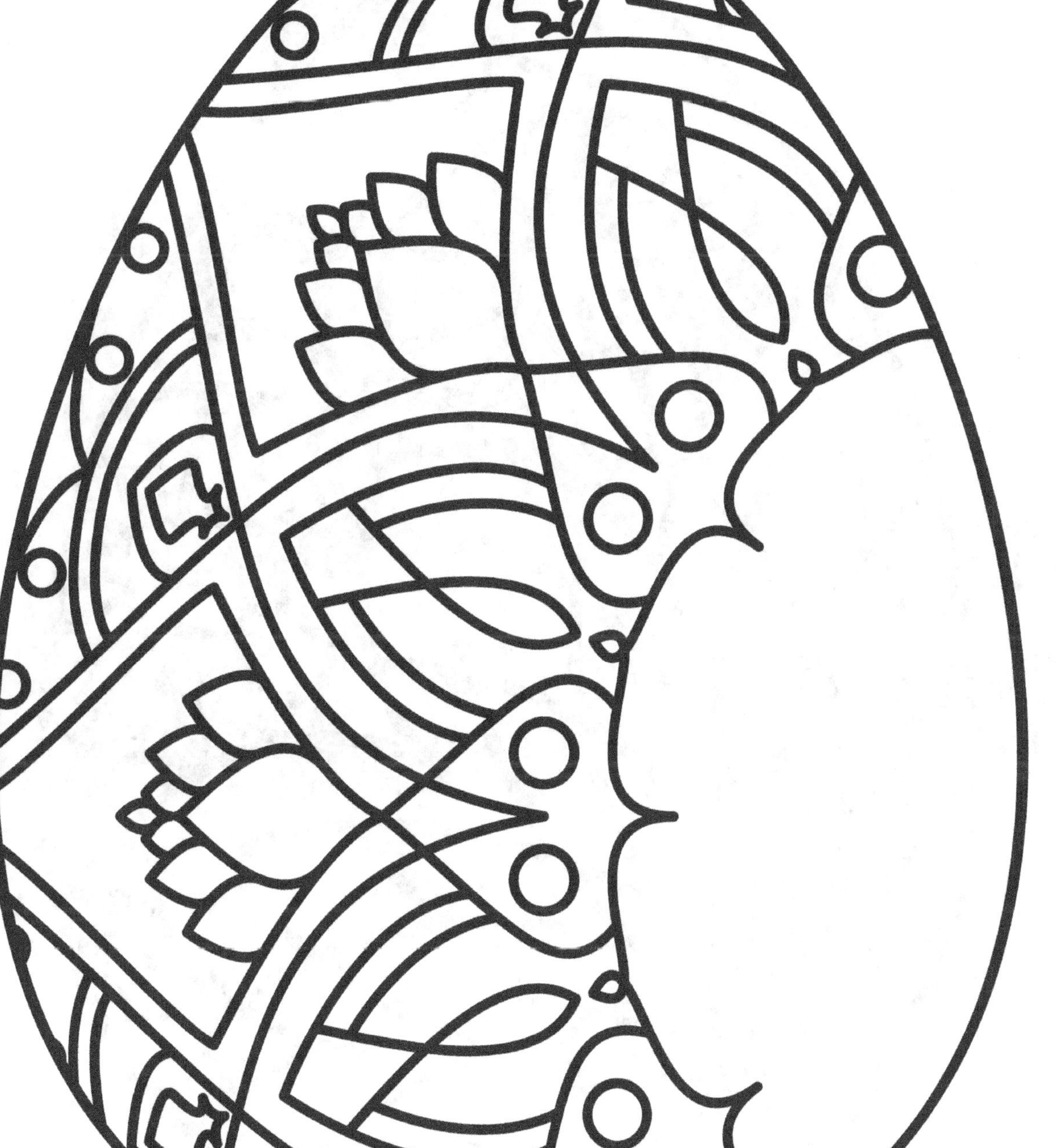

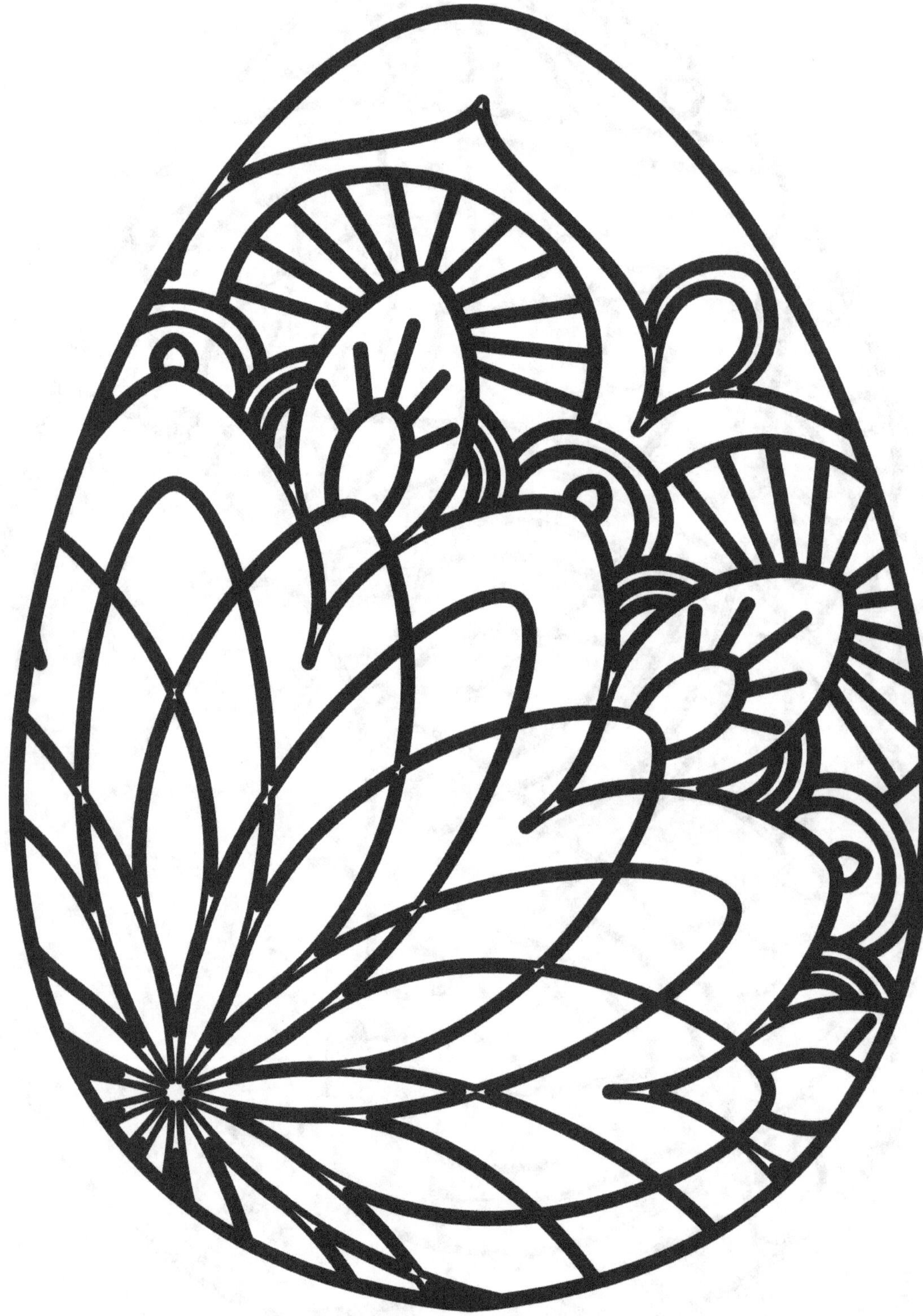

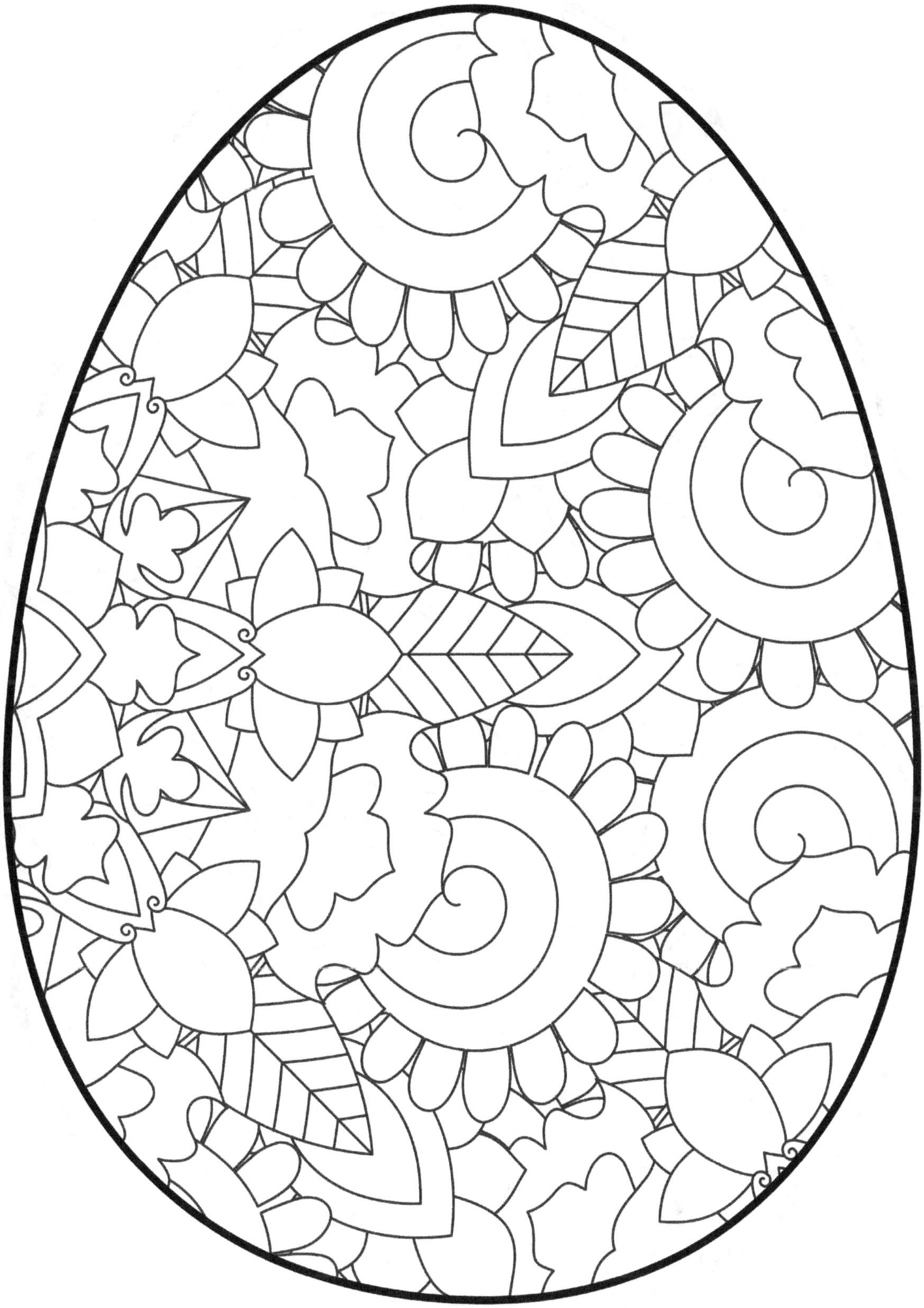

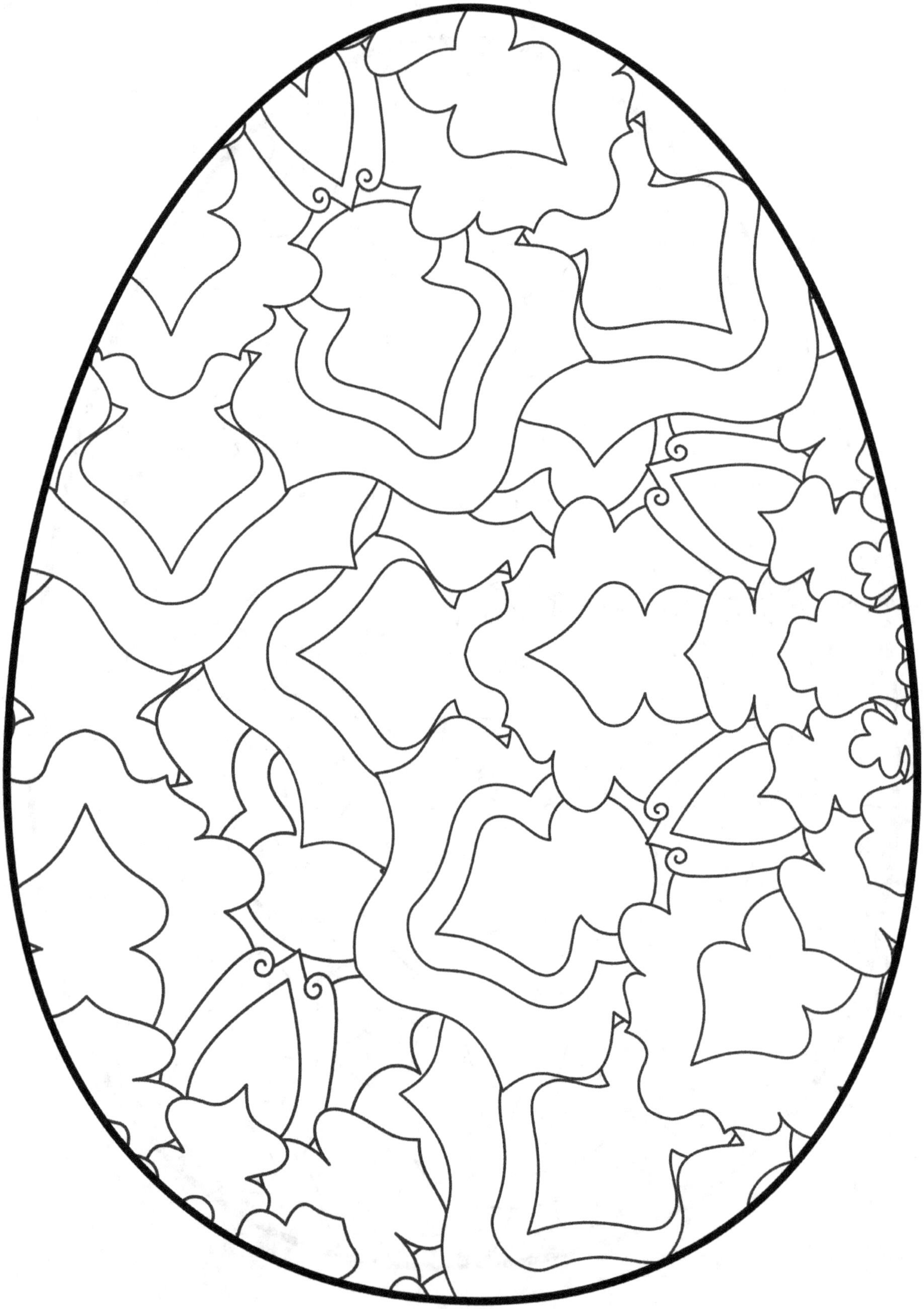

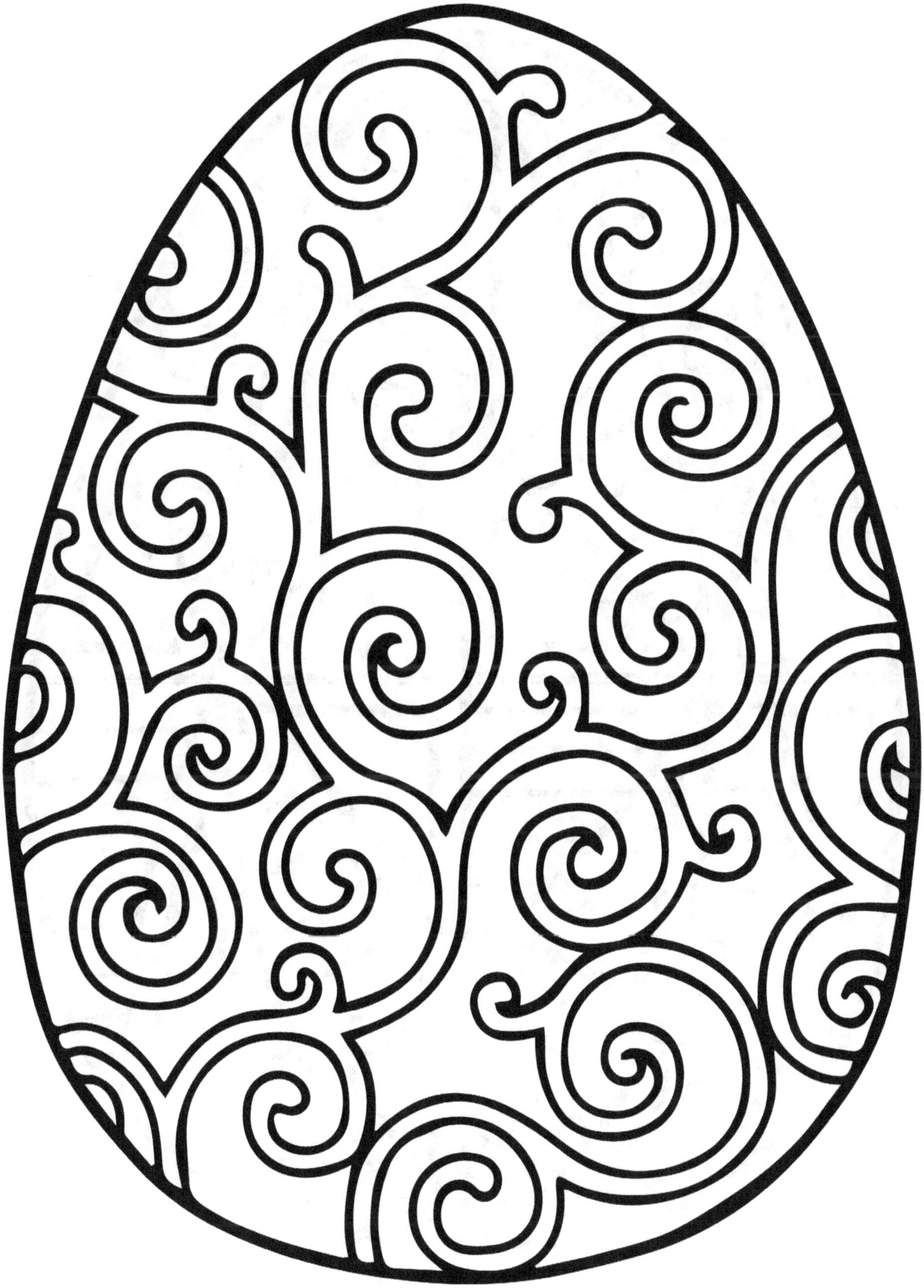

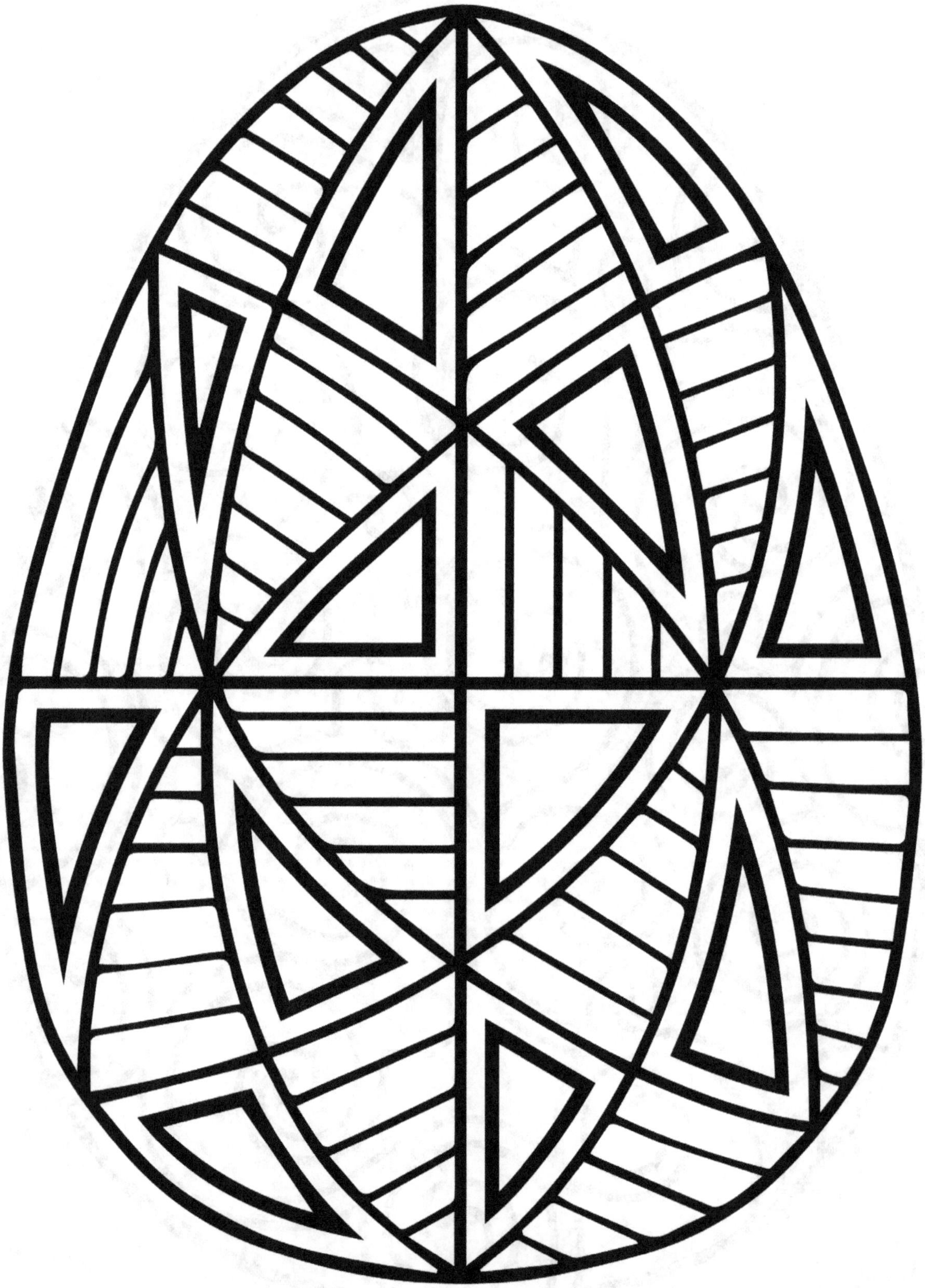

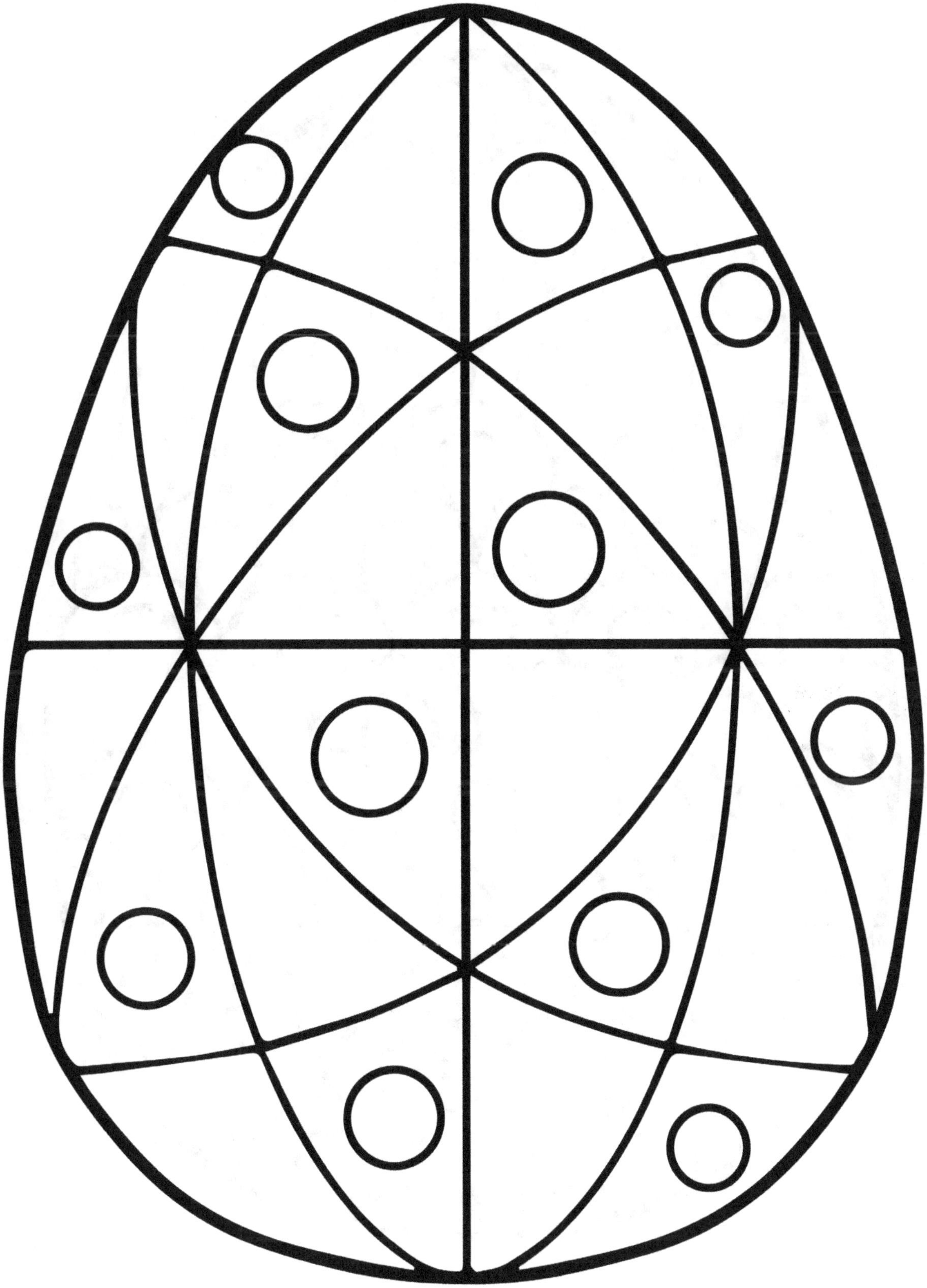

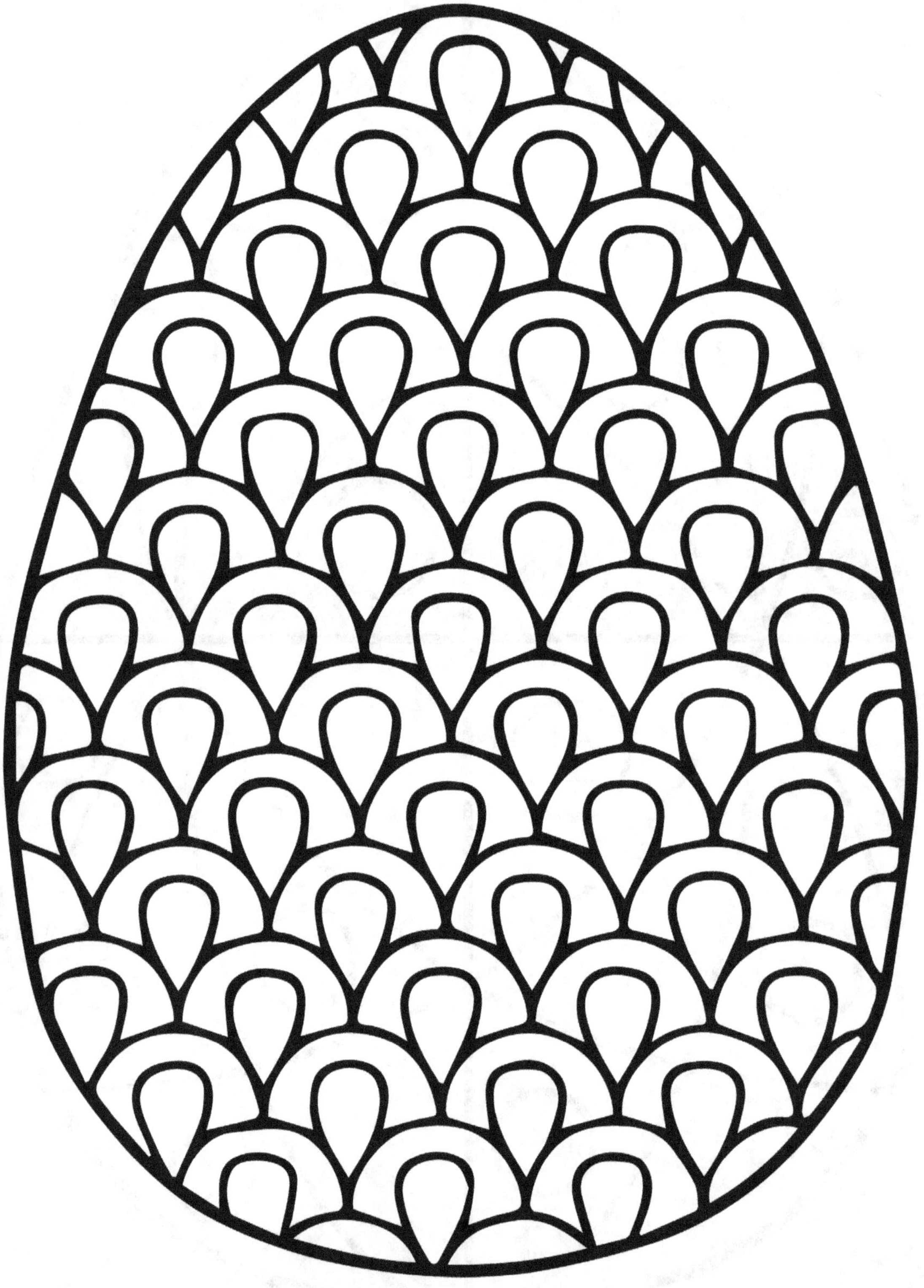

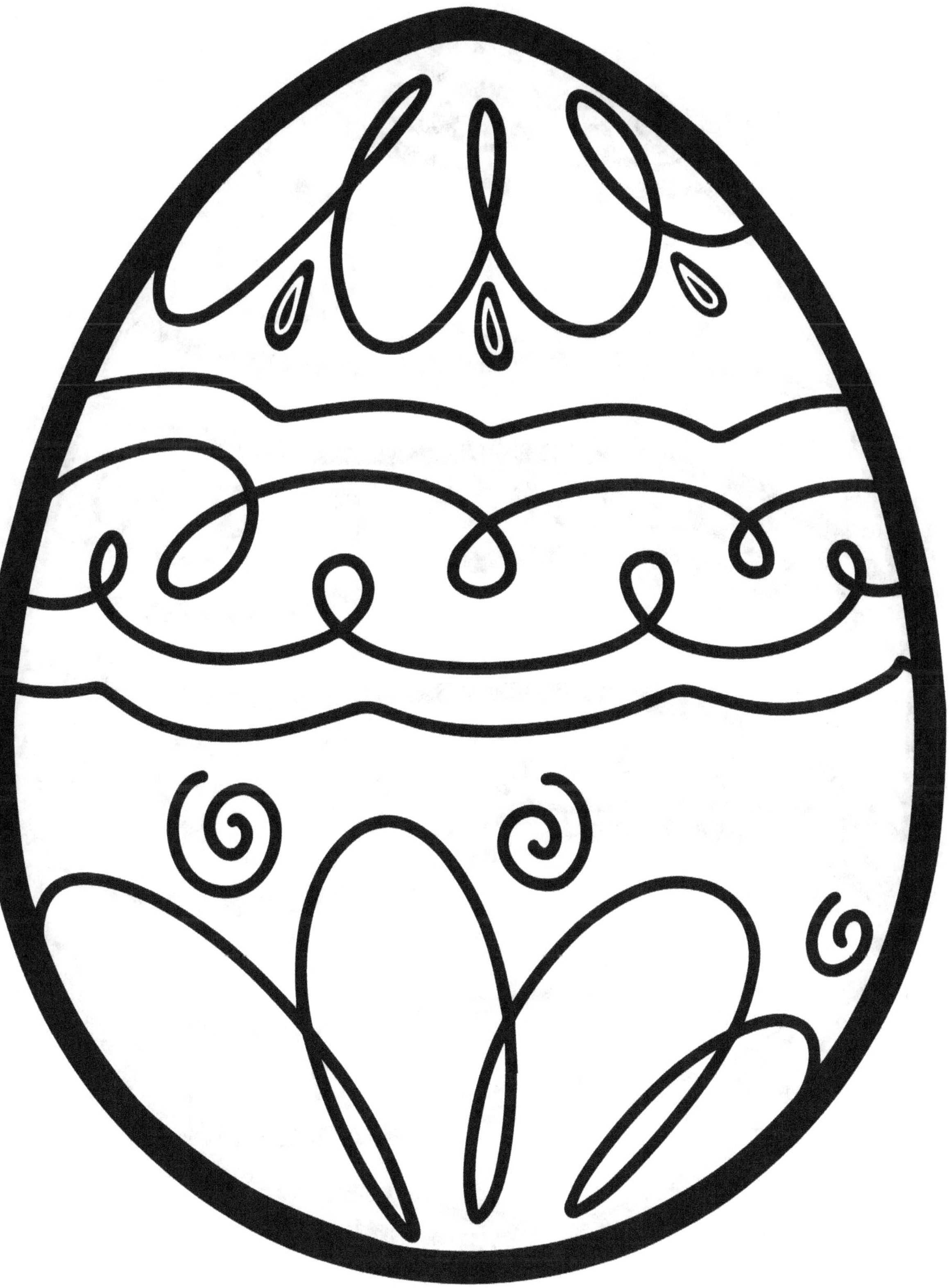

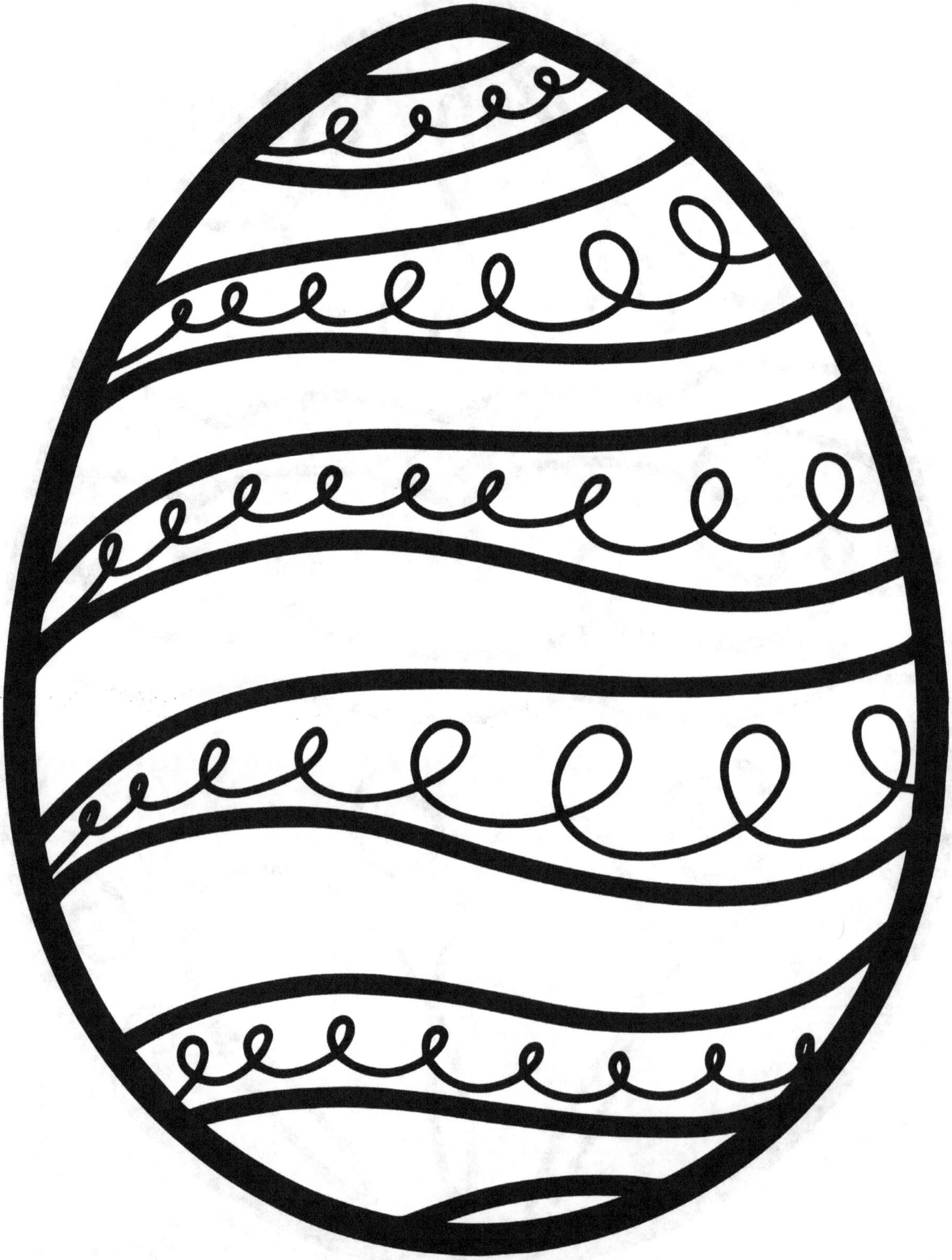

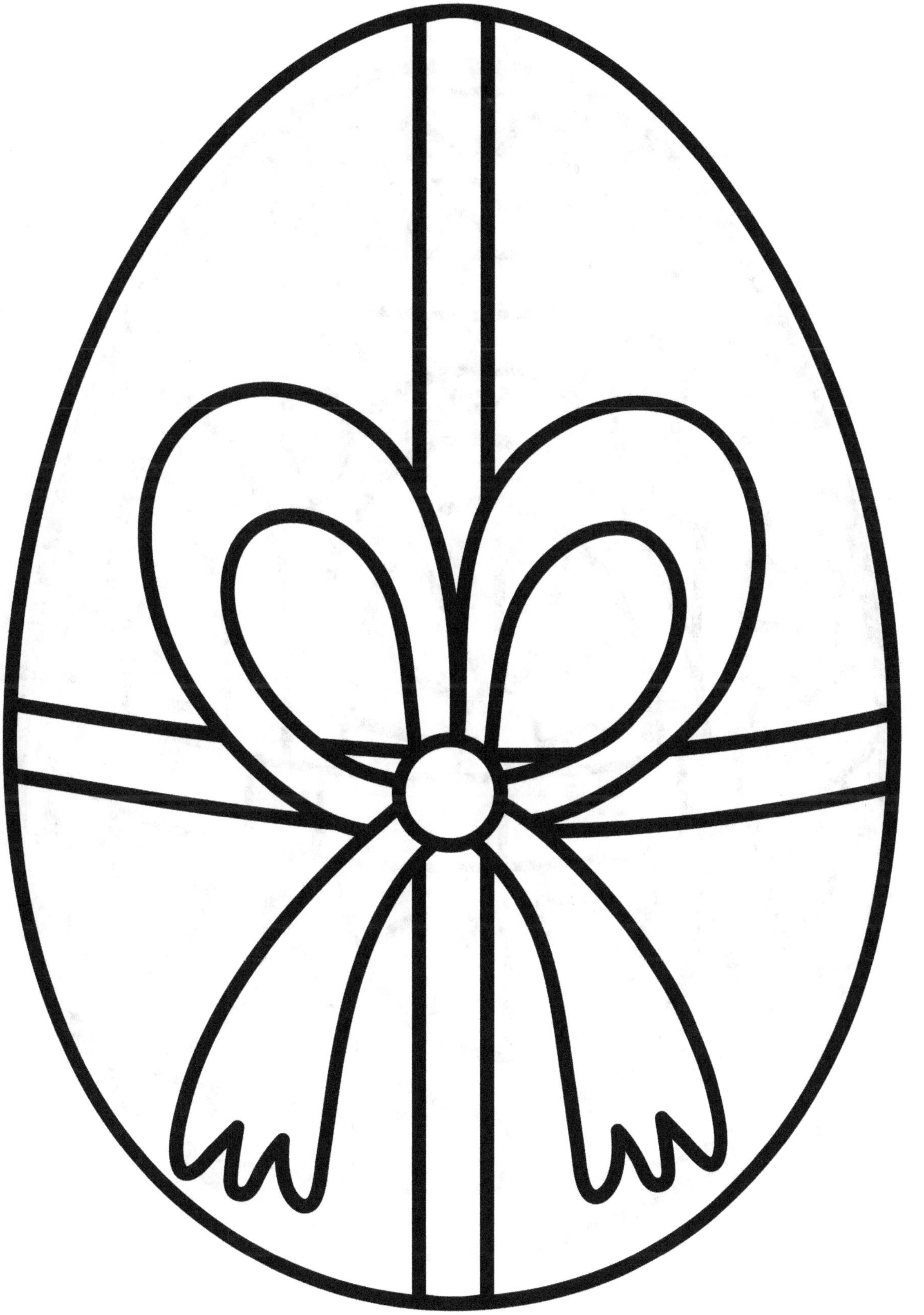

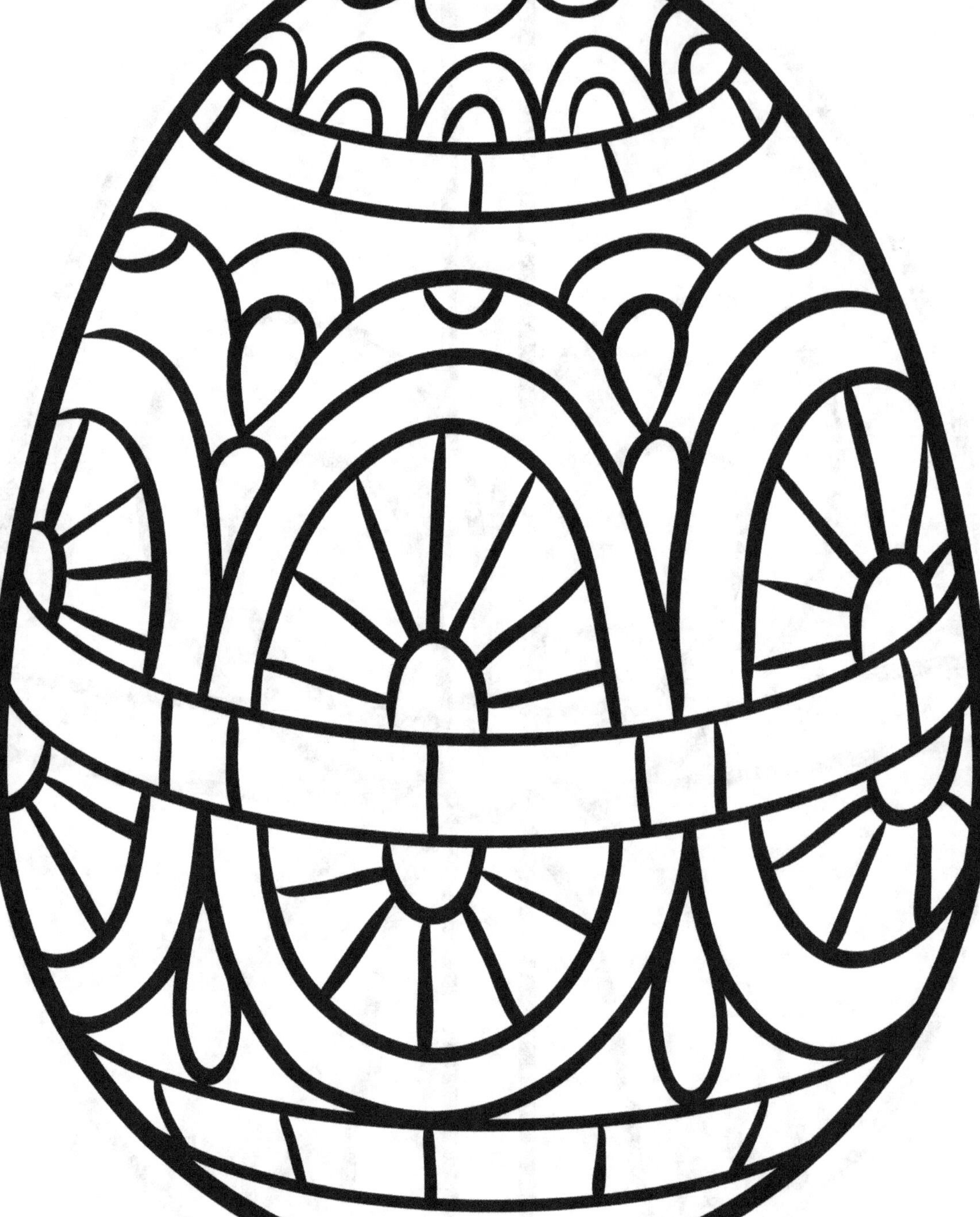

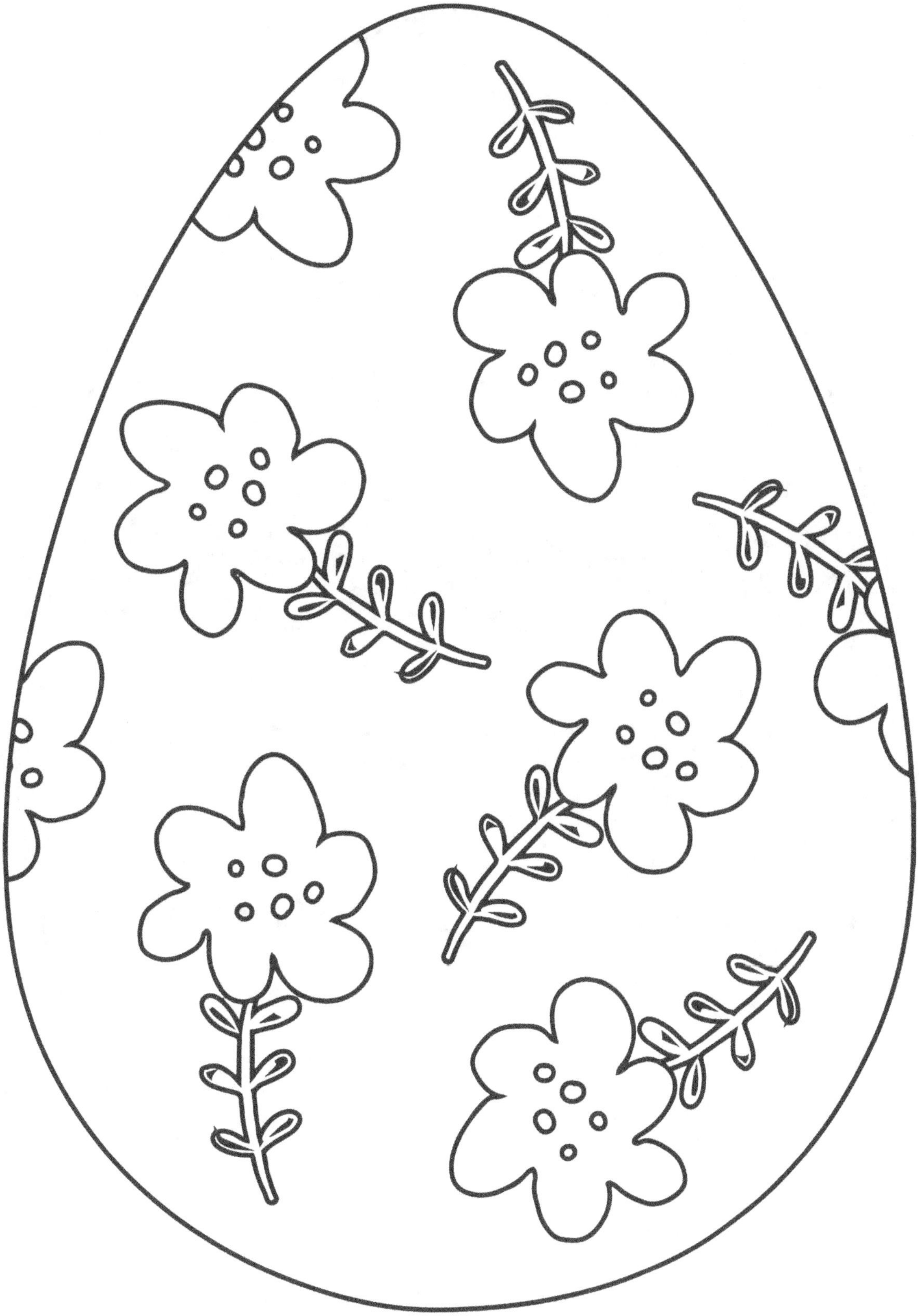

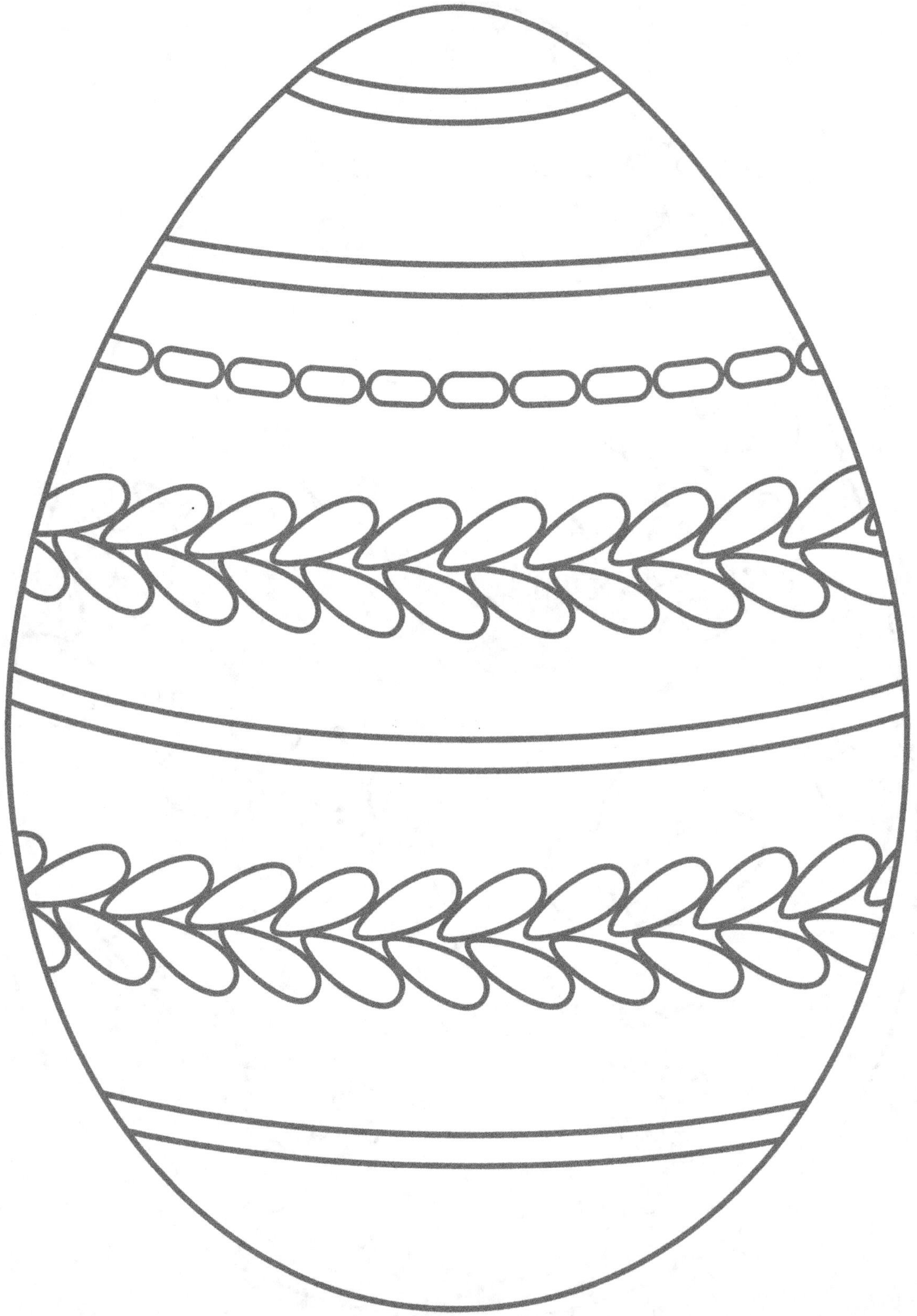

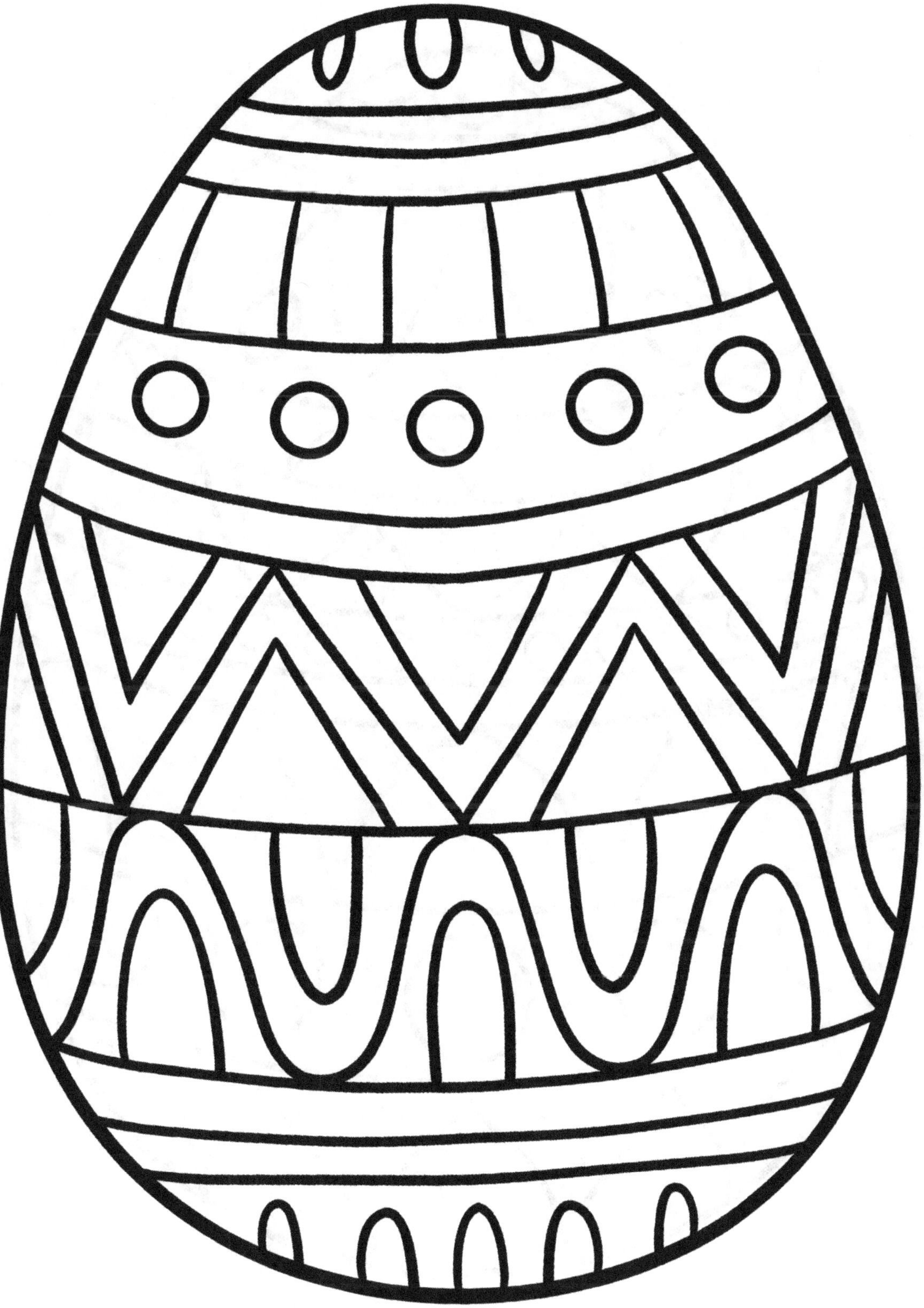

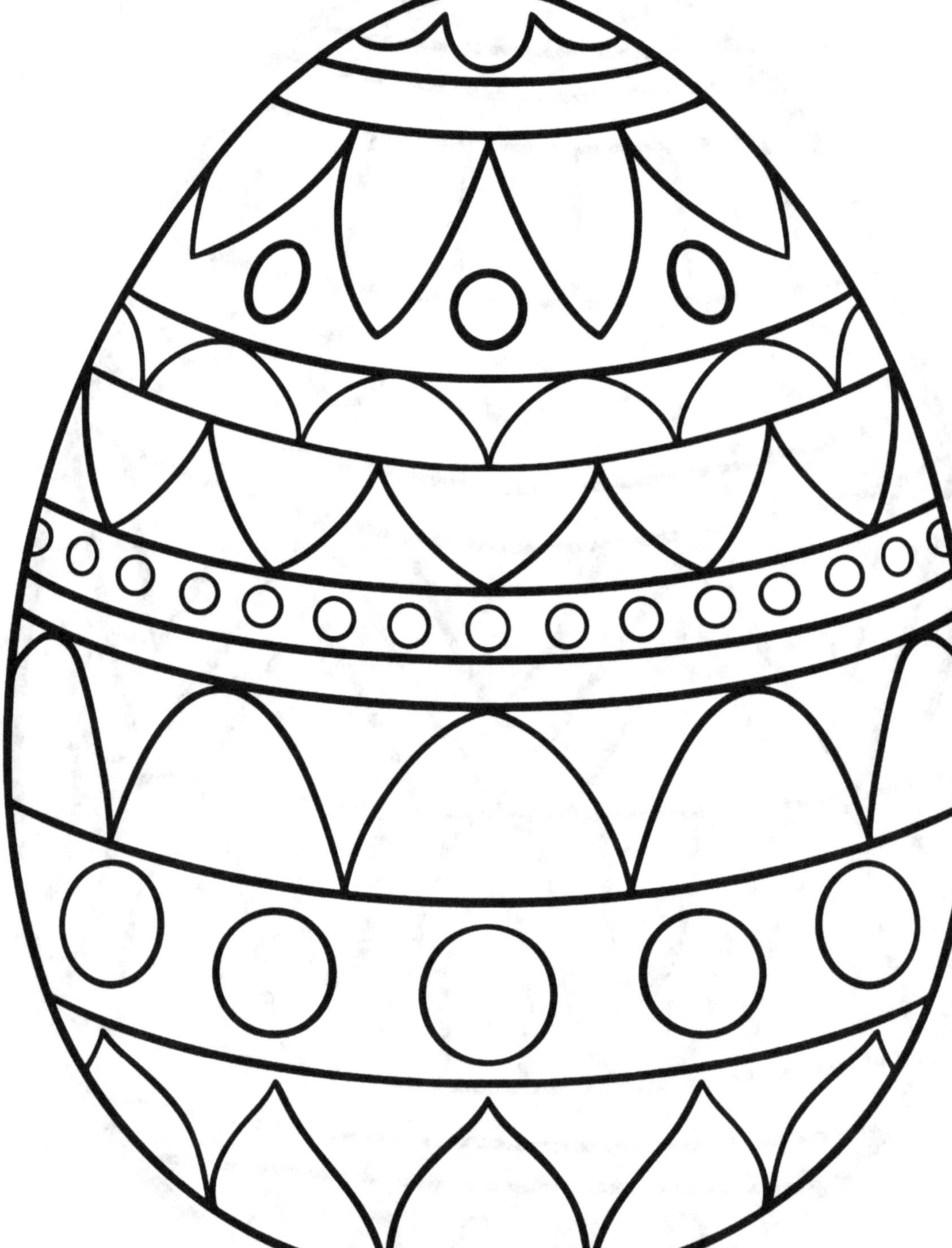

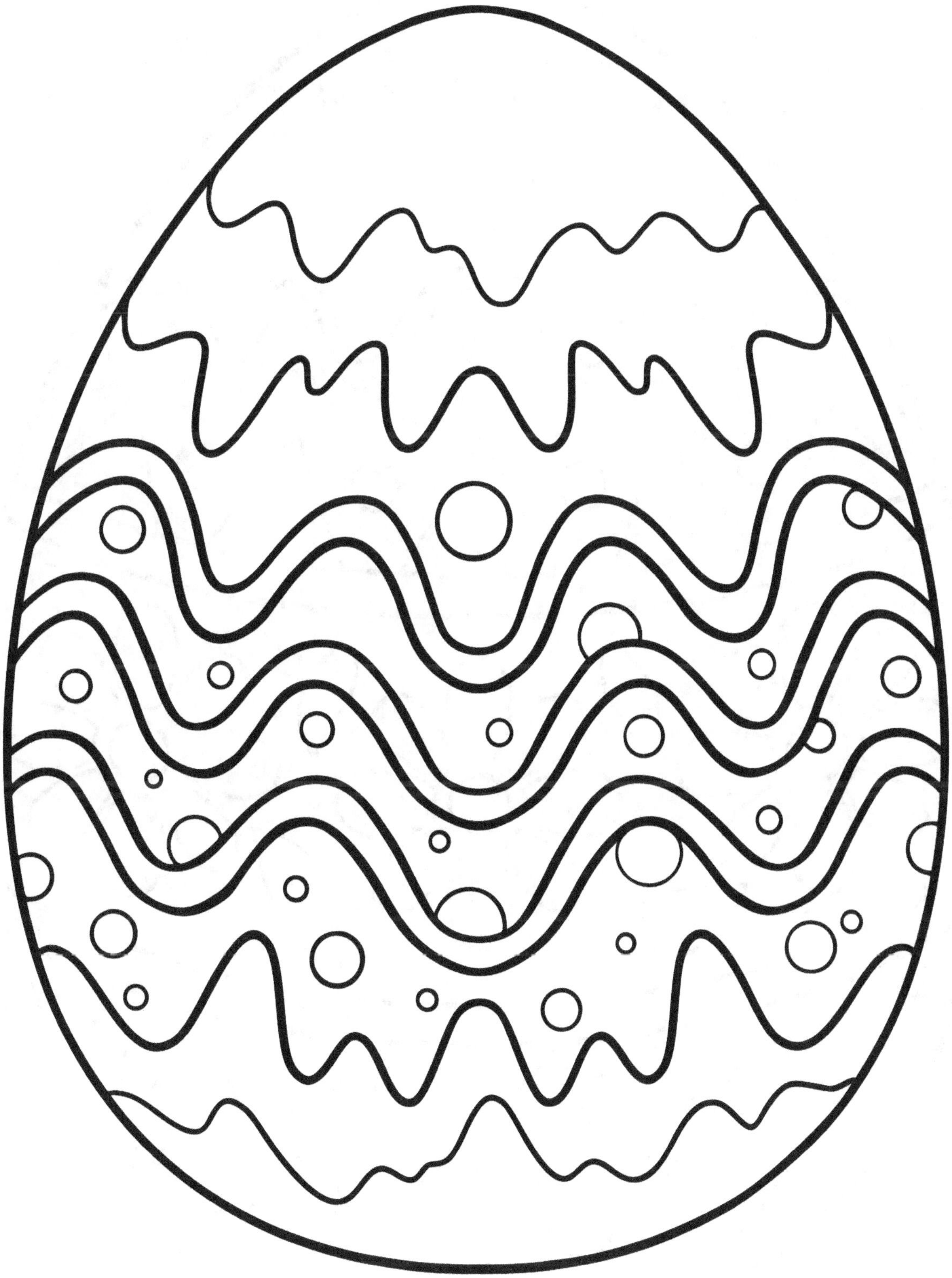

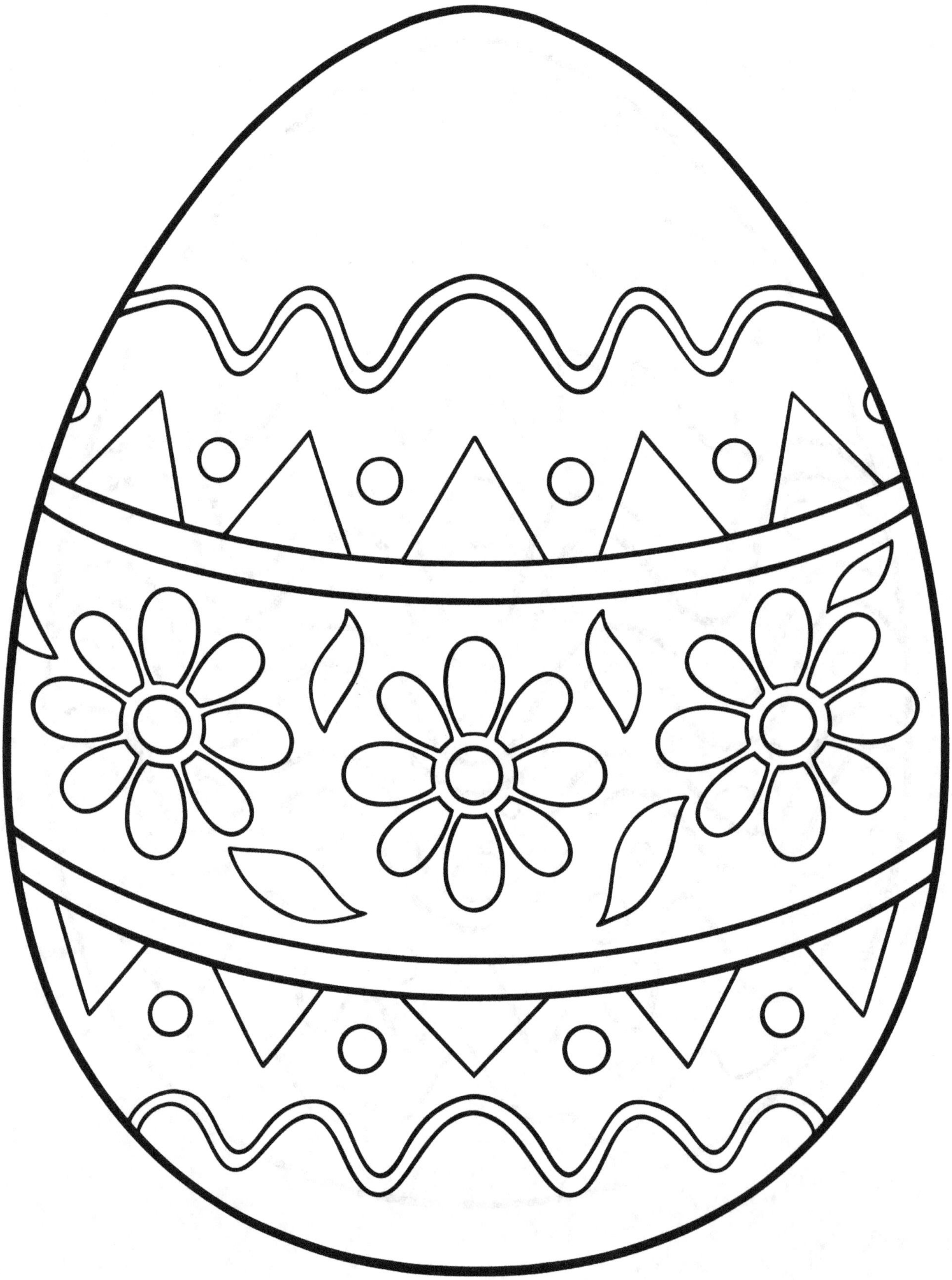

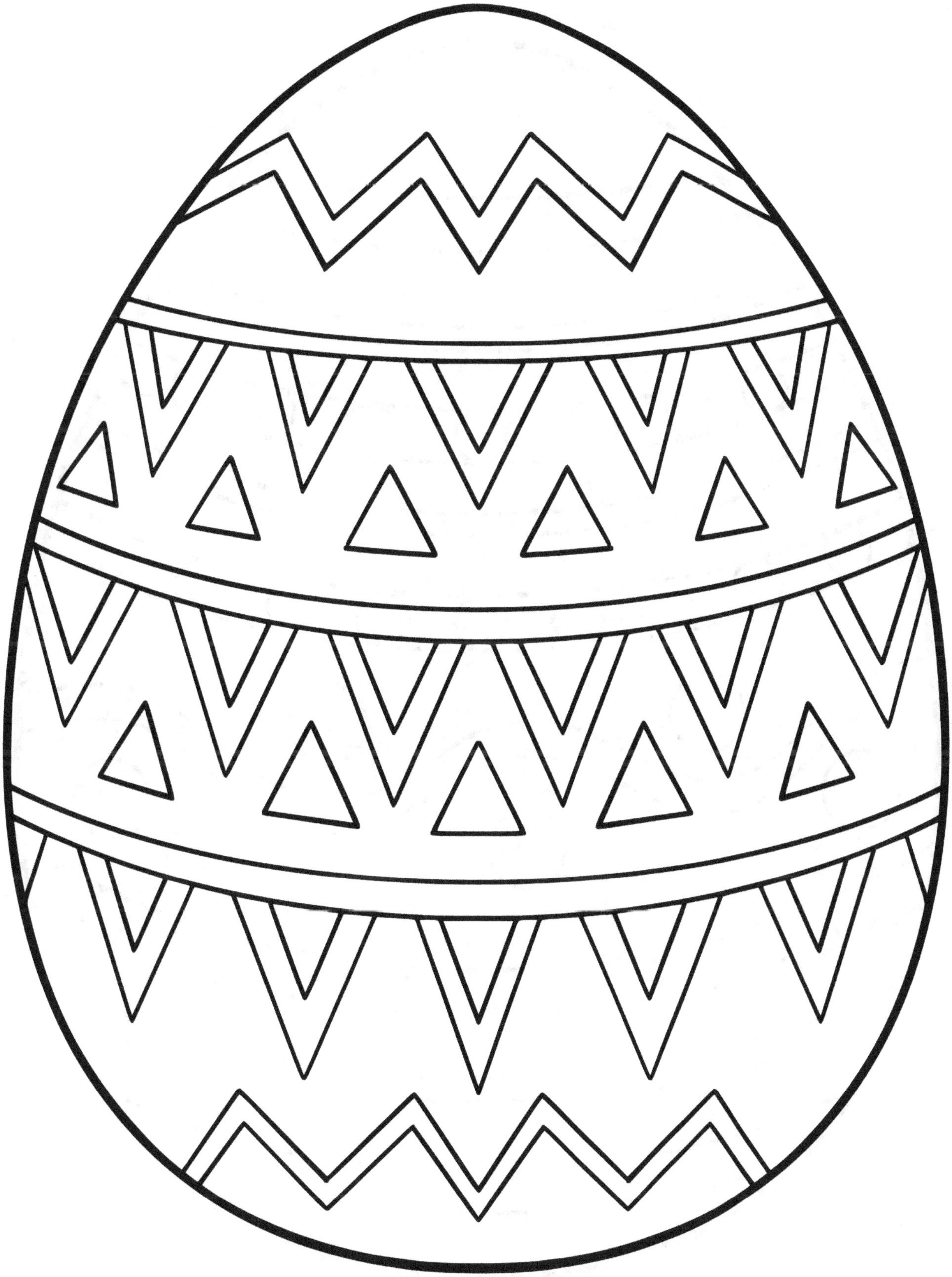

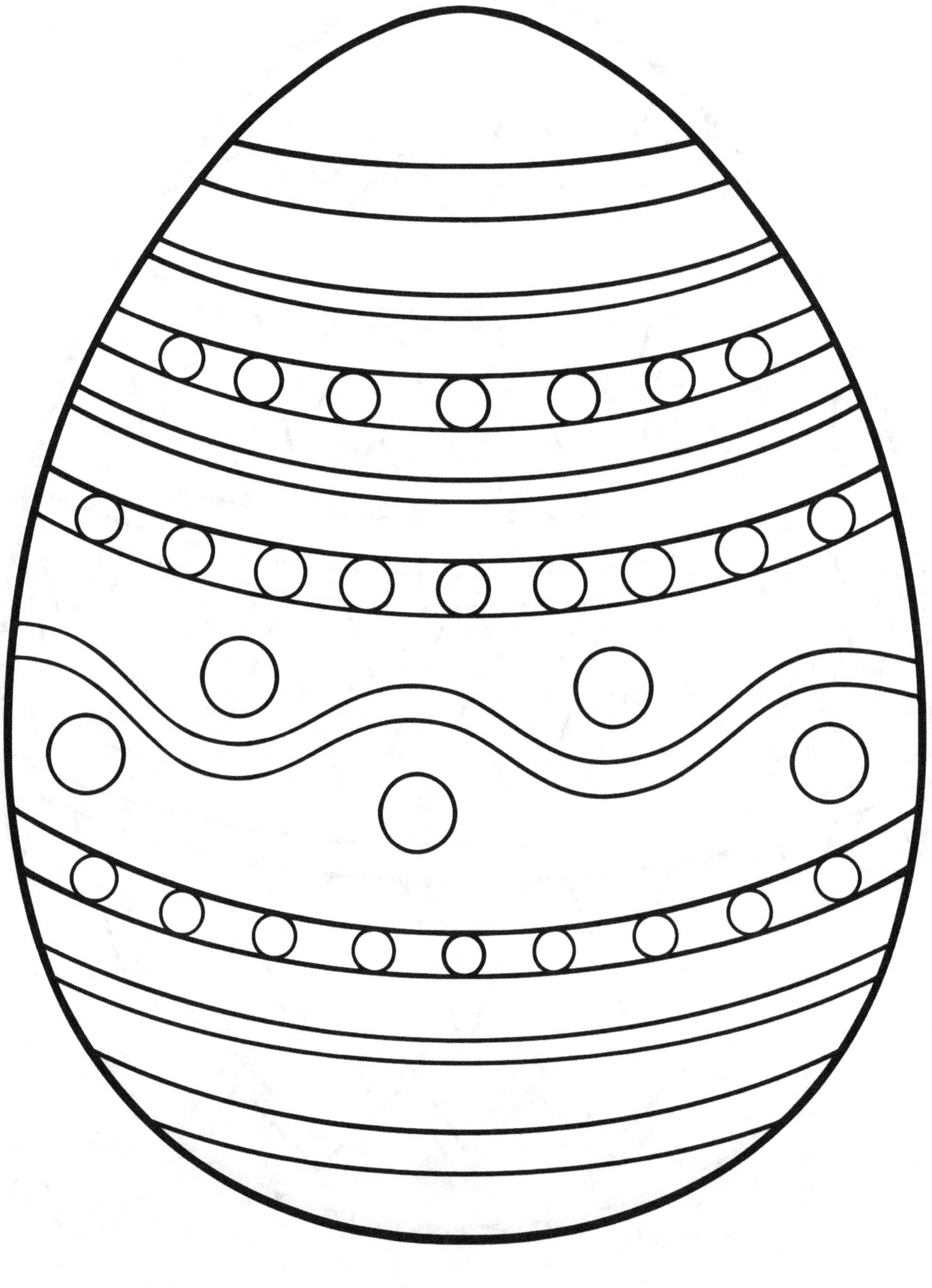

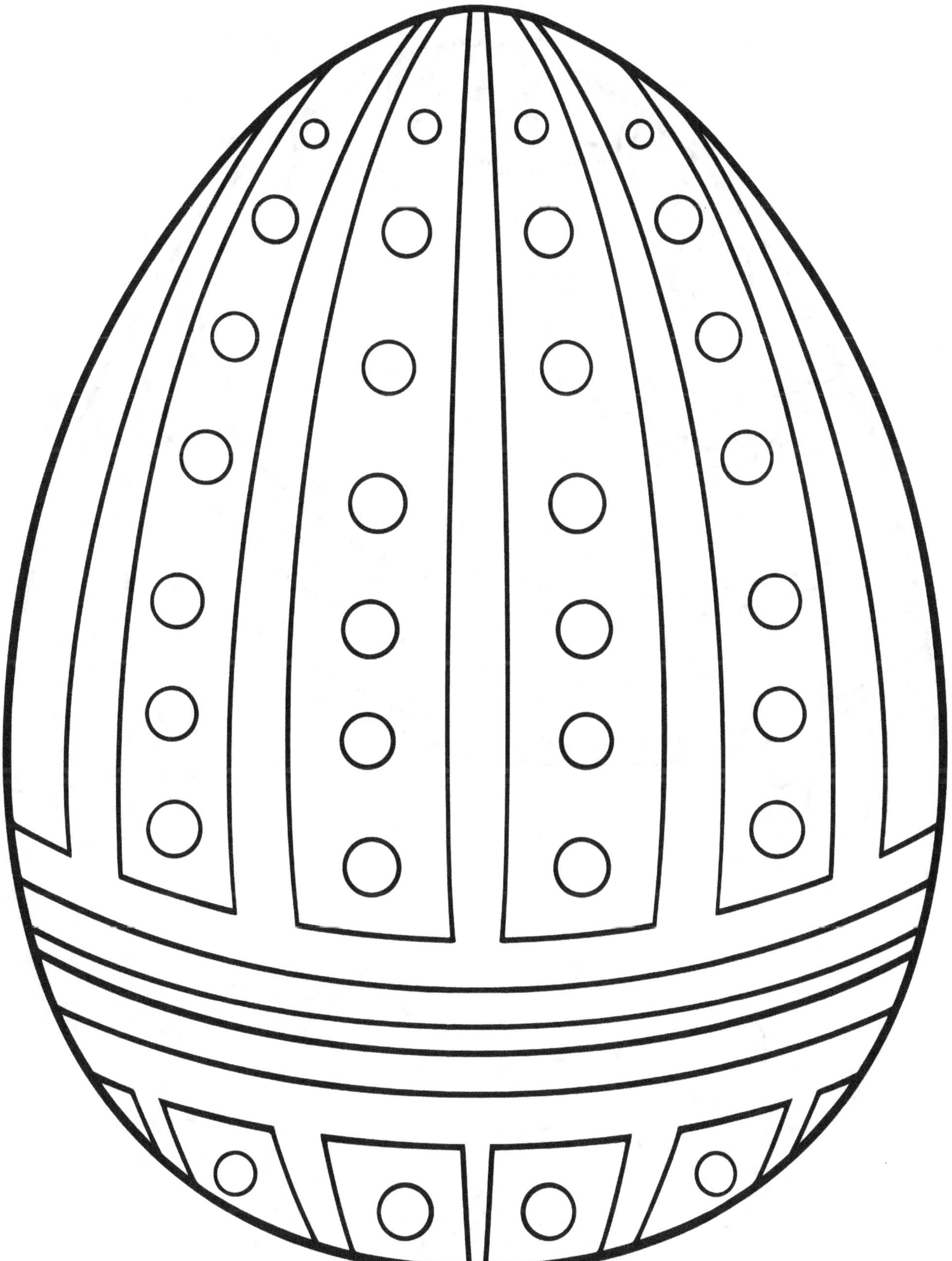

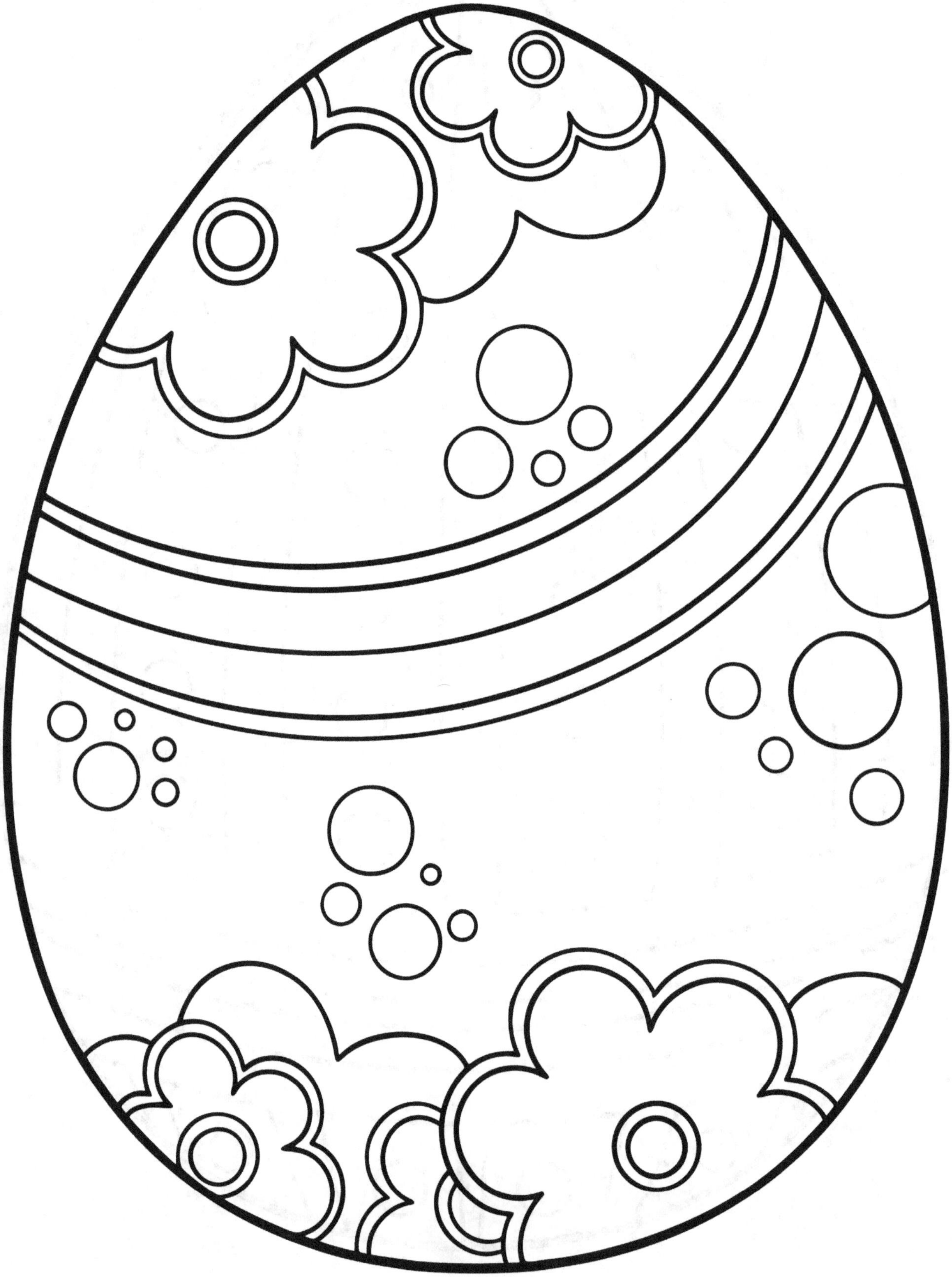

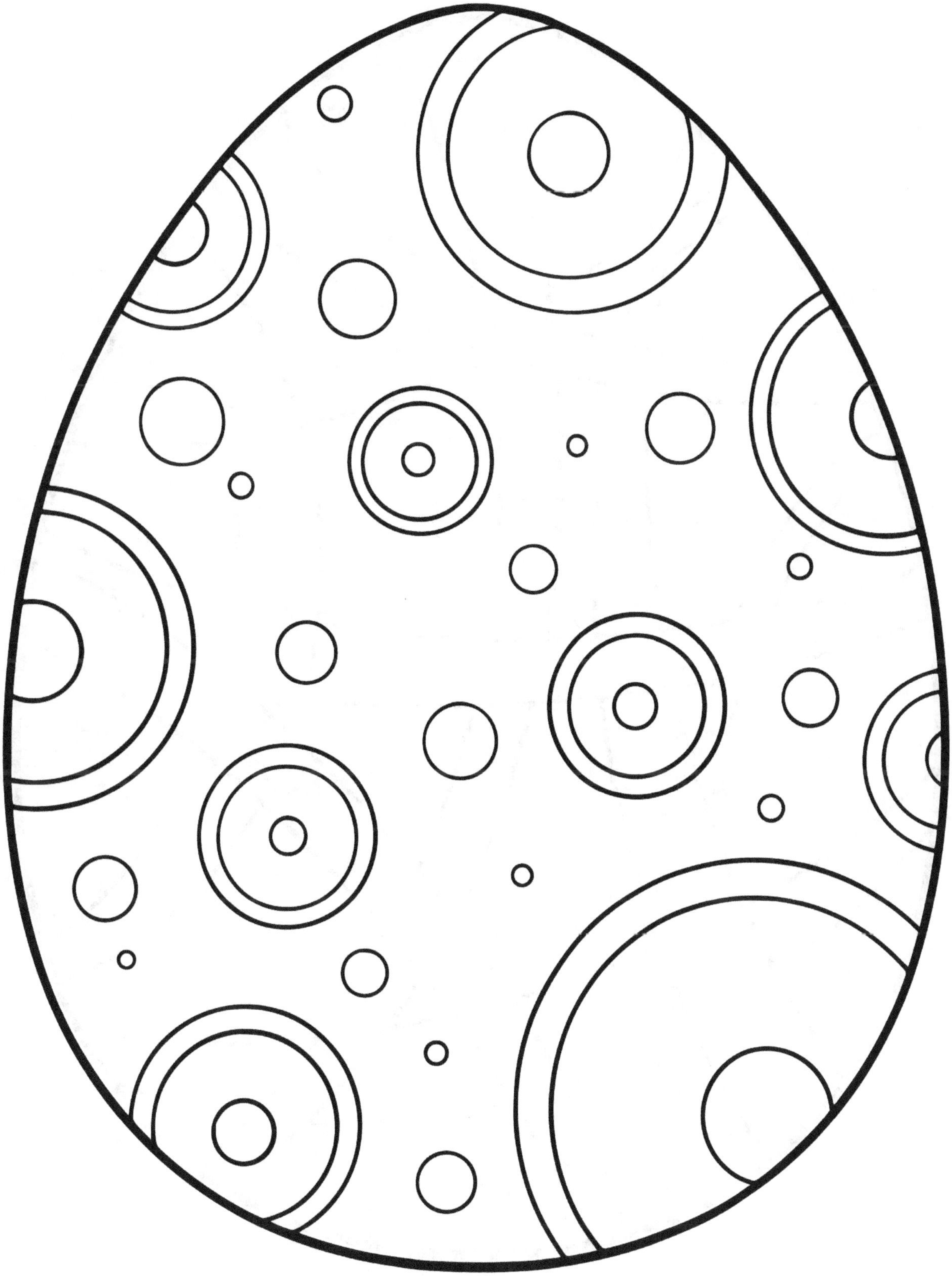

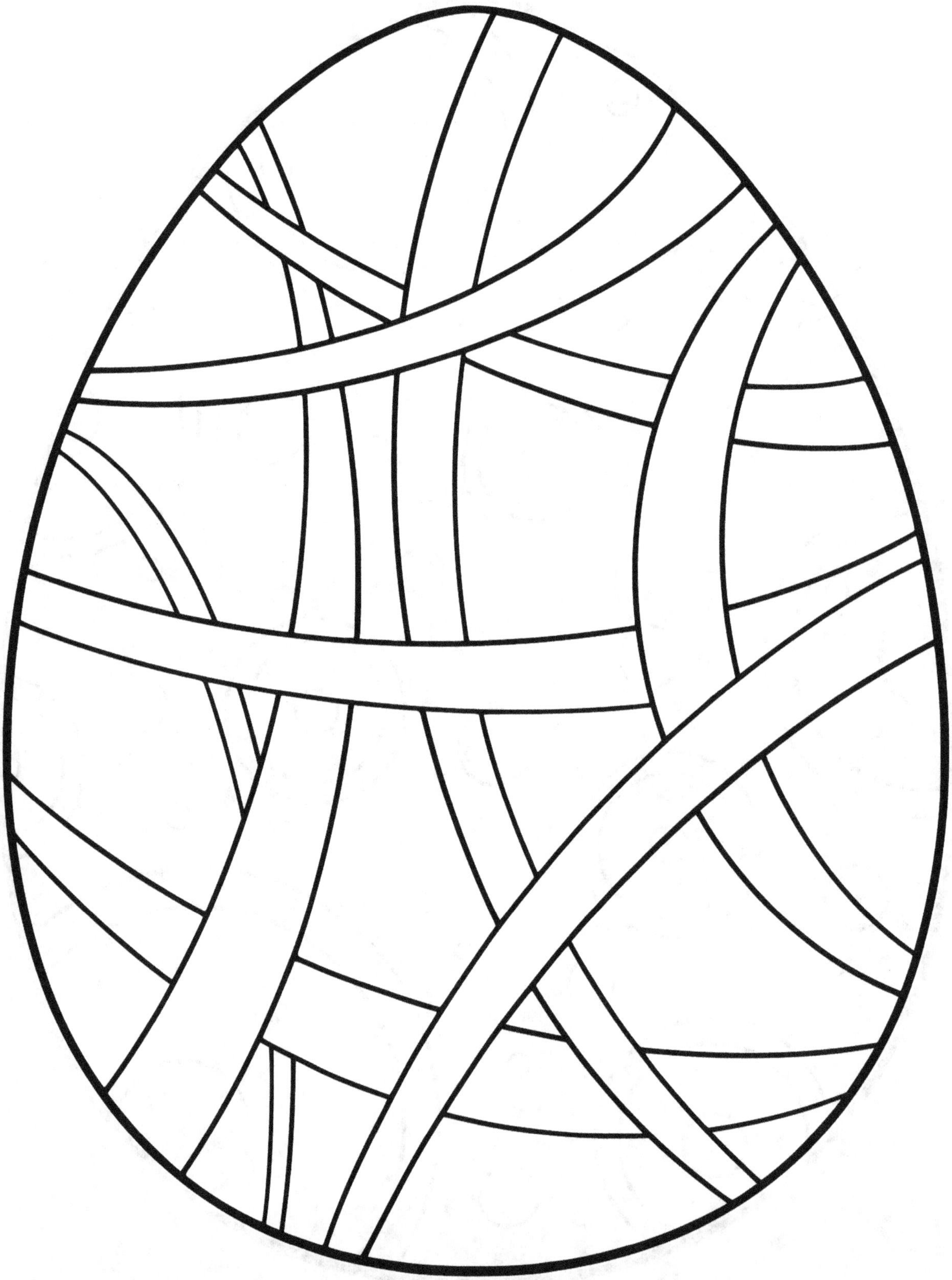

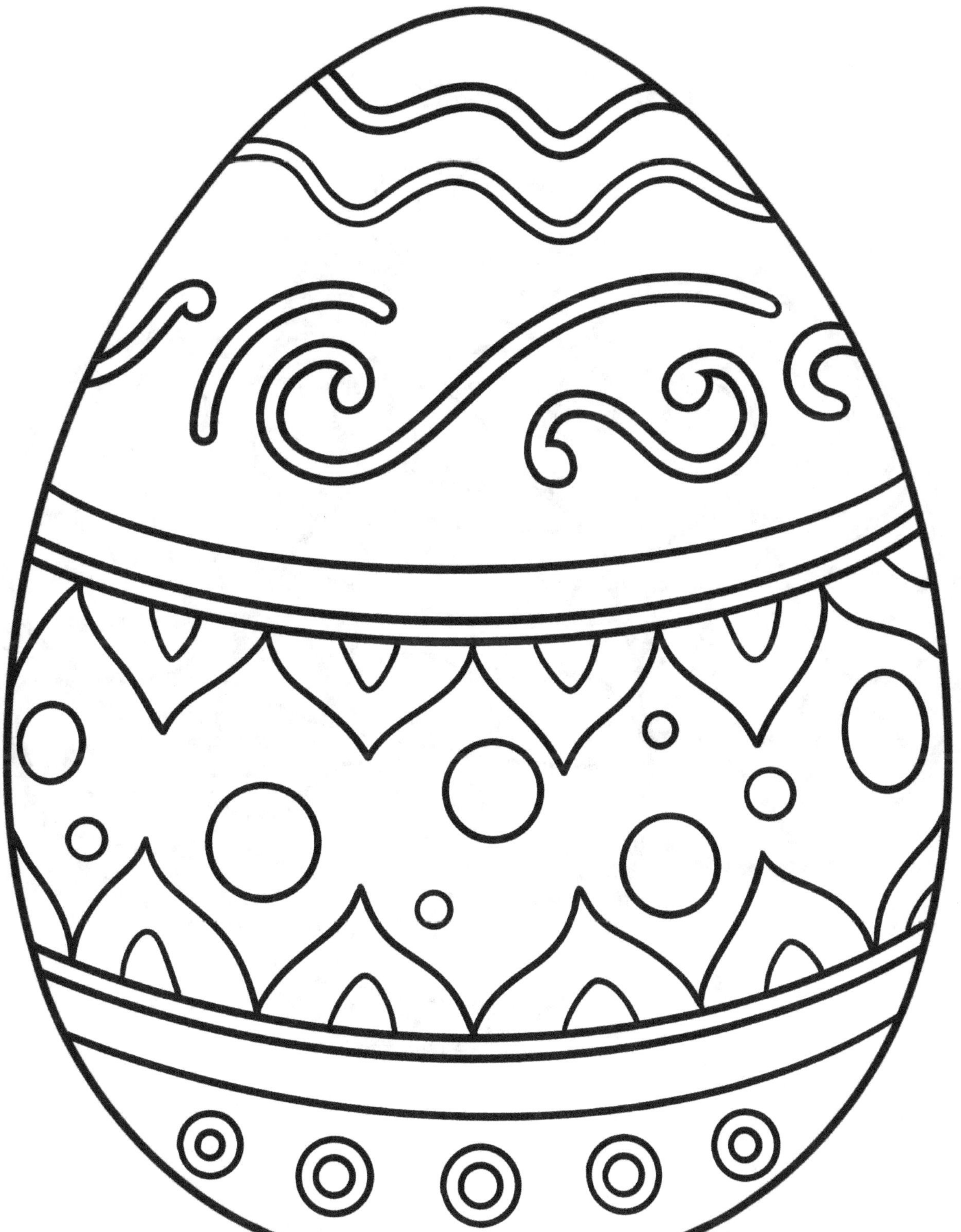

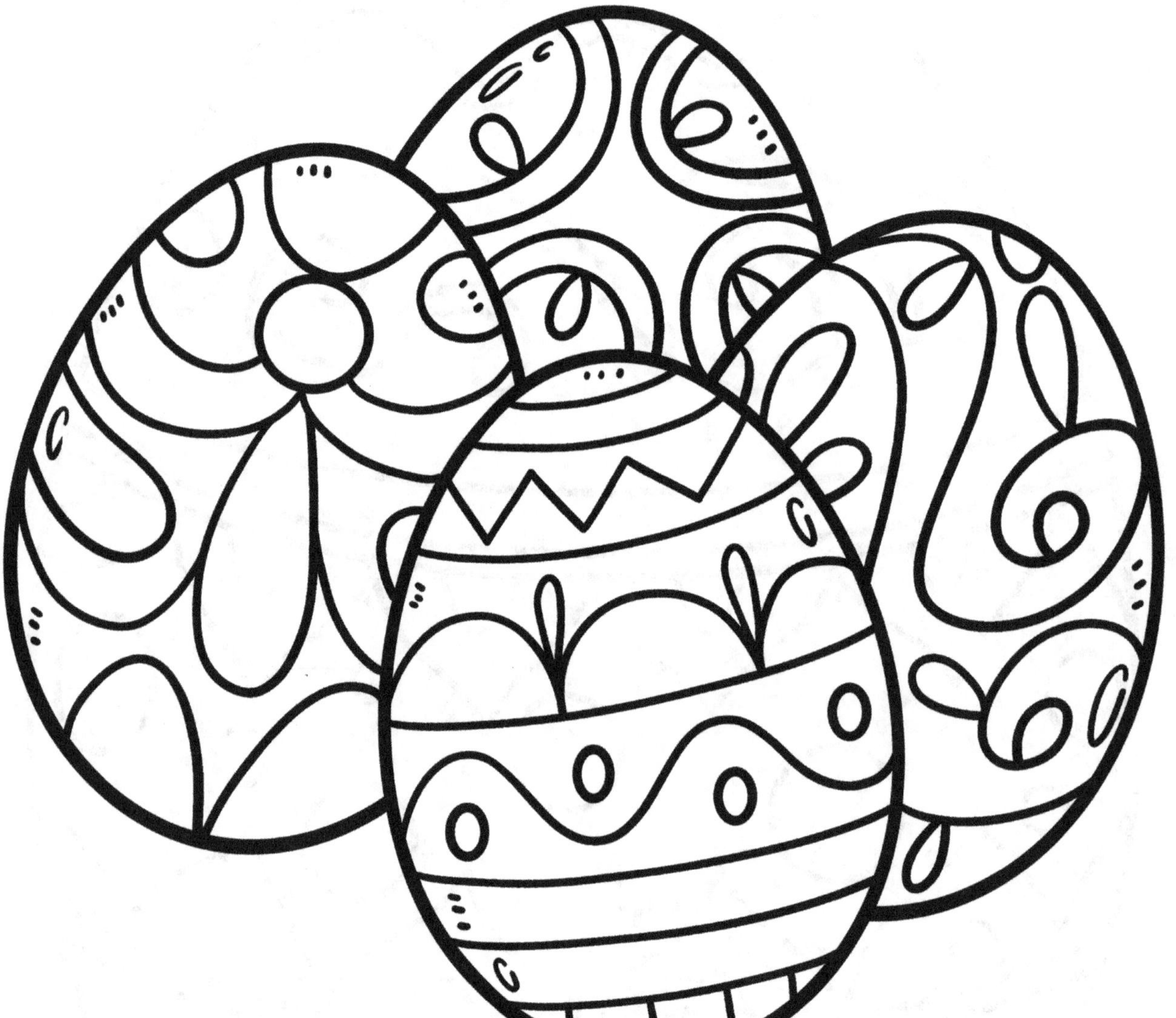

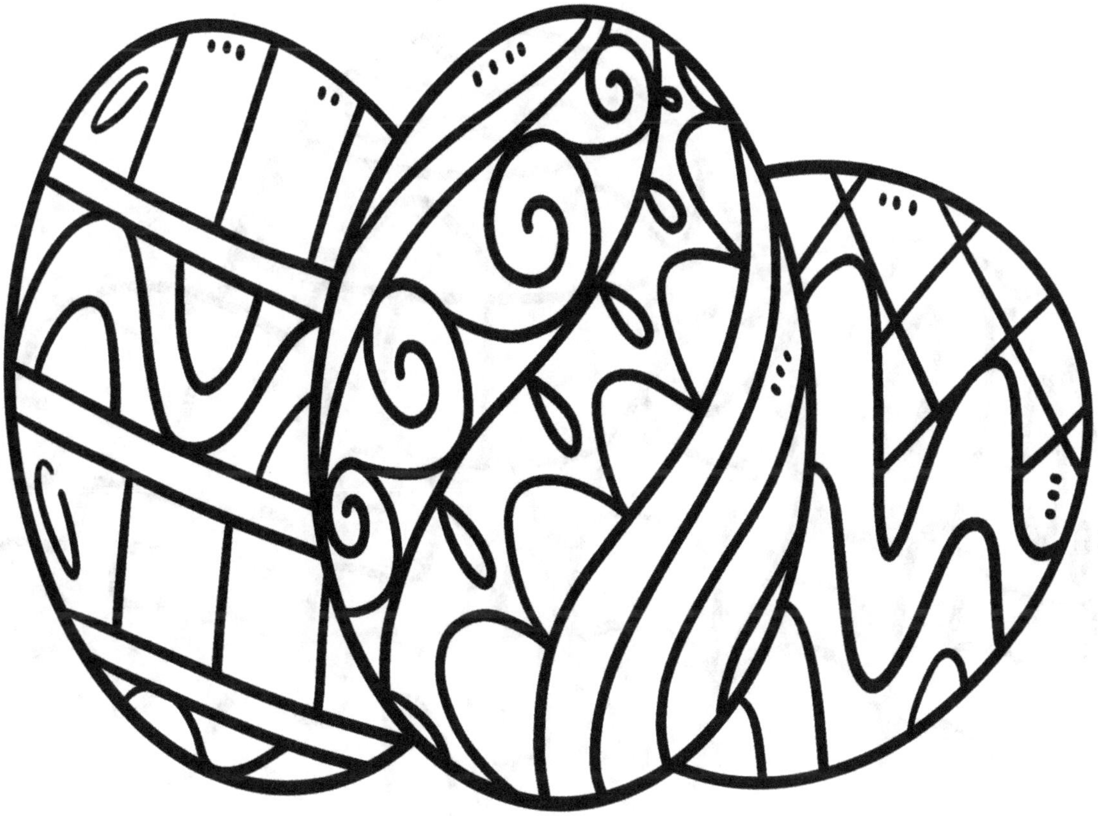

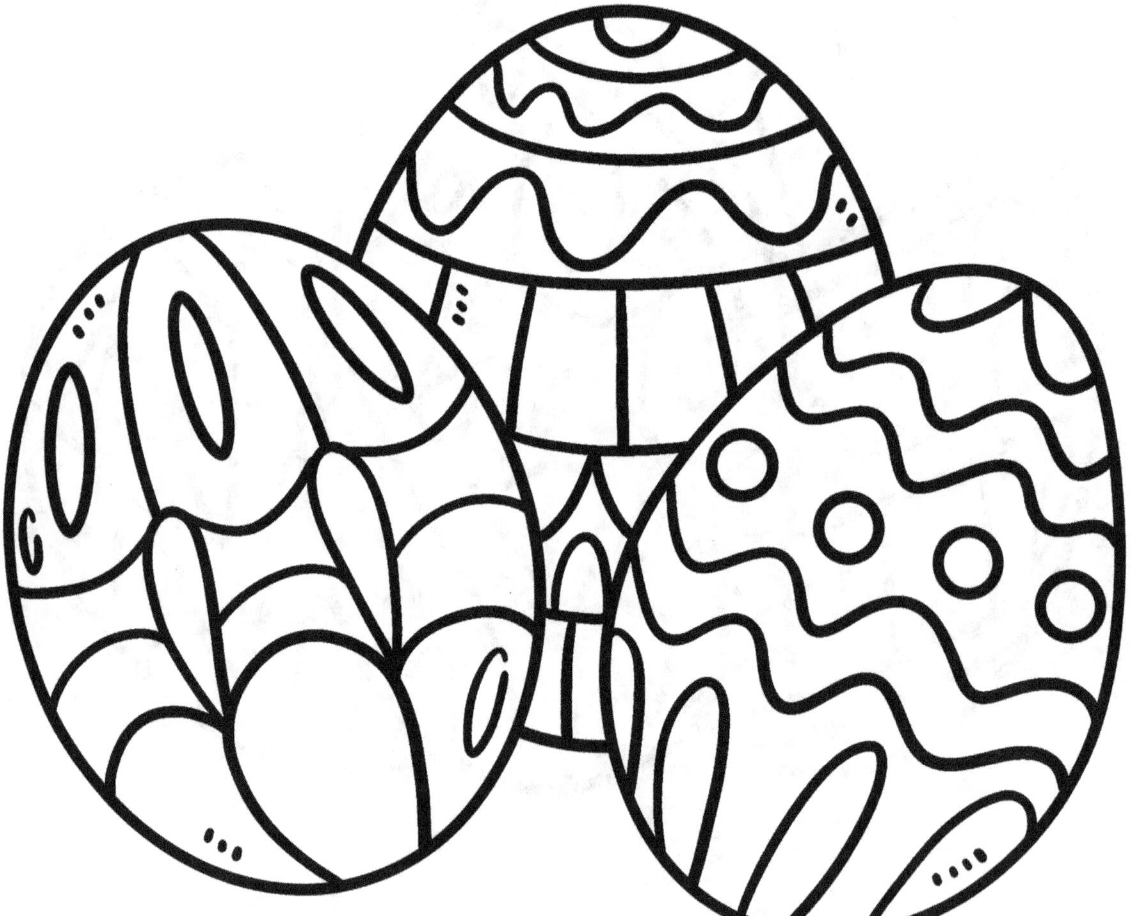

Happy Easter

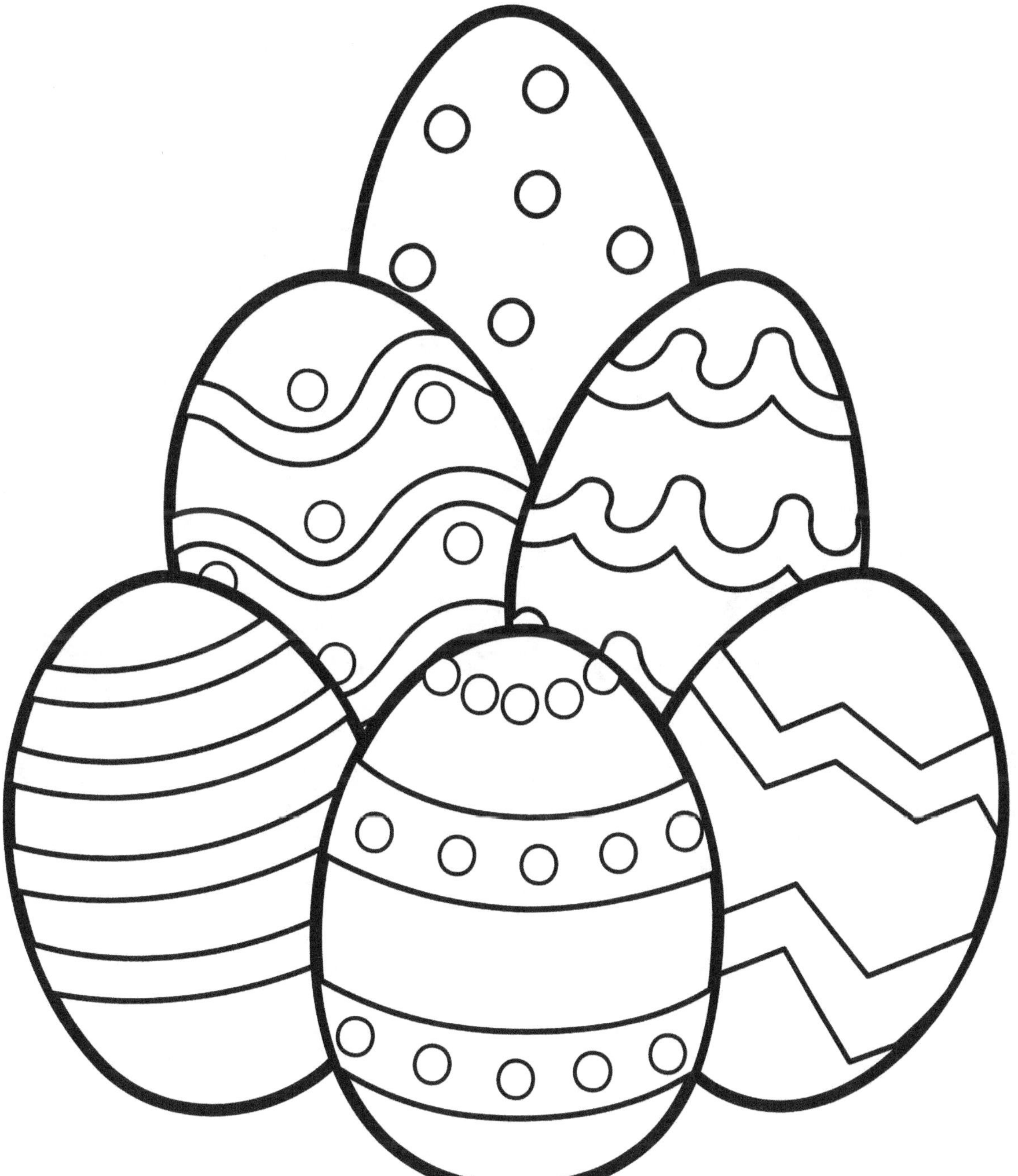

www.ingramcontent.com/pod-product-compliance
Lightning Source LLC
Chambersburg PA
CBHW080629220526
45467CB00011B/3437